CHURCH OF THE RESURRECTION OF CHRIST
(of the Saviour on the Spilled Blood)

It has long since been tradition in Russian architecture to erect religious buildings in honour of historic events. The Church in the Name of the Resurrection of Christ on the Site of the Mortal Wounding of His Honoured Majesty Alexander II, so the church's canonical title reads, stands on the exact spot where the emperor was fatally injured on 1 March 1881 by a bomb thrown by the radical, Ignaty Grinevitsky. It is more commonly known as the Church of the Saviour on the Spilled Blood. It would be more accurate, however, to call it the Church of the Resurrection on the Blood, since it was consecrated in the name of the Resurrection of Christ rather than in the name of Christ the Saviour. This striking edifice is one of the few remaining examples of late 19th – early 20th century religious architecture in Russia and today represents a commemorative monument of both historic and artistic value.

What events preceded the tragic drama that was played out on the bank of the Catherine Canal? What were the reasons behind the lamentable death of the Russian autocrat otherwise known as the Tsar-Liberator who had done so much for the country entrusted to his care?

1. The Coronation of Alexander II in the Dormition Cathedral in the Moscow Kremlin. 1855,
State Museum of the Moscow Kremlin.

On 15 February 1855, Emperor Nicholas I died suddenly. The shame of defeat in the Crimean War played a significant part in the death of the great autocrat. His son, Alexander, inherited a heavy load, including the lost but as yet unfinished Crimean War, social unrest and increasing talk of emancipation among the serfs. The demise of a once great nation seemed imminent. When he came to the throne, Alexander declared a truce, putting an end to the bloody Crimean War of 1853–1856. It was only after this that his coronation was held, and it was then that the first of the terrible omens that seemed to prevail over the reign of Alexander II was noted. During the coronation ceremony in the Dormition Cathedral in the Moscow Kremlin, an elderly courtier fainted and dropped the cushion bearing the orb. The spherical symbol of autocracy resonated as it hit the ground and rolled across the stone floor...

Under Alexander II, the country began to experience significant changes and unprecedented reforms: the judicial system was reformed, a system of local administration under the so-called zemstvos was introduced, military service was reorganised, the rules of censorship were revised, and – most importantly – the peasants were liberated from serfdom.

An active foreign policy was also implemented. Russia ended the protracted war in the Caucasus and, with the aid of a subtle diplomatic policy, restored its rights to the Black Sea. It extended its boundaries, adding Kars and Batum to its lands and reclaiming part of Bessarabia that had previously been ceded. Among other things, it also campaigned for the liberation of the Balkan Christians.

Alexander II signed the manifesto on the abolition of serfdom on 19 February 1861. "Today is the best day of my life", said the tsar, while the writer, Alexander Herzen, dubbed him the "Liberator". However, the reform turned out to be half-hearted. Having waited for their freedom for so many years, the serfs were disappointed when it was finally

granted without bringing them entitlement to the land itself. As a result, a wave of agrarian disturbances swept across the country, while the more radical members of the intelligentsia summoned antiquated Russia to the executioner's block, threatening to exterminate thousands of landowners along with the royal family.

On 4 April 1866, Dmitry Karakozov fired a shot at Alexander II by the railings of the Summer Garden in St Petersburg. This failed assassination attempt put an end to the era of the "great reforms", which gave way to a period of police repression. On the crest of the country's mounting internal political crisis, a party known as "Narodnaya Volya" ("The Will of the People") was born. It waged open war on the state authorities and literally declared Alexander II a wanted man. On 26 August 1879, at a congress in Lipetsk, party members pronounced the death penalty for the emperor. Between 1879 and 1881, eight assassination attempts were made. One fortune-teller came terrifyingly close to the truth when she predicted that the tsar would die during the seventh attempt on his life. On a number of occasions, terrorists sought to derail the imperial train and laid mines along the routes that the emperor's cortege was to follow through the city. On 2 April 1879, five shots were fired at Alexander II at almost point blank range on Palace Square and it was only by sheer chance that they did not hit their target. On 5 February 1880, Stepan Khalturin and Andrei Zhelyabov masterminded an act of terrorism inside the Winter Palace itself. Several of the rooms of the imperial residence suffered as a result and the floor of the Imperial Dining Room was damaged. As luck would have it, Alexander II was at the other end of the palace at the time. The flaming ring of terror slowly tightened around the emperor. Nonetheless, shortly before his death in January 1881, he signed a proposal to admit elected delegates from towns and provinces to the State Council. However, on 1 March 1881, on the eve of the publication of the imperial decree that would have signalled the beginning of constitutional government in Russia, Alexander II was killed. The explosion from the bomb thrown by the Narodnaya Volya member, Ignaty Grinevitsky, tore off the emperor's legs as he was alighting from his carriage to

2. *The Royal Family.*

3. *Alexander and his parents, Emperor Nicholas I and Empress Alexandra Fyodorovna.*

4. *The Manifesto of 19 February 1861.*

5. *Emperor Alexander II in his study.*

БОЖІЕЮ МИЛОСТІЮ

МЫ, АЛЕКСАНДРЪ ВТОРЫЙ,

ИМПЕРАТОРЪ И САМОДЕРЖЕЦЪ

ВСЕРОССІЙСКІЙ,

ЦАРЬ ПОЛЬСКІЙ, ВЕЛИКІЙ КНЯЗЬ ФИНЛЯНДСКІЙ,

и прочая, и прочая, и прочая.

Объявляемъ всѣмъ НАШИМЪ вѣрноподданнымъ.

4

5

3

6

7

Часовня Лѣтняго сада.   С.-Петербургъ.

8

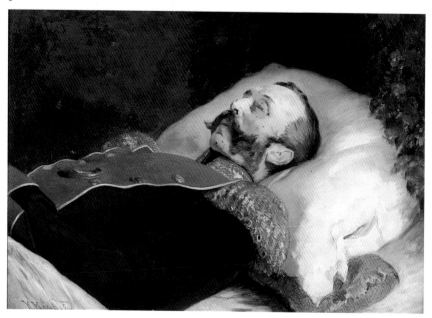

9

speak words of encouragement to the Cossacks in his escort who had been wounded by a missile thrown only moments previously by Nikolai Rysakov. Alexander II and his assassin died at the same time, one in the Winter Palace from blood loss, and the other in the prison hospital.

So it was that the revolutionary terror that led to the death of the tsar-reformer hindered the emergence of representative government in Russia. The country's evolutionary development was suspended. Who knows what course the development of Russia would have taken if a constitutional monarchy had been established at that time...

Alexander III, who came to the throne after the death of his father, ordered that a church be erected on the spot where the emperor had been killed, in order to remind "the hearts of those who look upon it of the martyrdom of the deceased Alexander II, and to evoke the loyal sentiments of devotion and grief experienced by the people of Russia". On 27 April 1881, the Petersburg Duma's so-called Committee for the Immortalisation of the Memory of Alexander II announced a competition for the creation of a church. The emperor was unmoved by the initial proposals and expressed the desire that "the church be built in the purely Russian style of the 17th century", in keeping with the traditions of the architecture of "great and orthodox Rus'." Herein lay one of the defining characteristics of Alexander III's reign, an era that took as its motto the principals of the official concept of nationality that were first established during the reign of Nicholas I: "Autocracy, Orthodoxy, Nationality." The tsar's terms became paramount for those who made it to the final round of the competition. Of the many works submitted, the emperor finally selected a project by the architect Alfred Parland (1842–1919).

The basic plan of the church in the form of the five open petals of an immortelle was the brainchild of the abbot of the Trinity–St Sergius Monastery (Lavra), Archimandrite Ignatius (Ignaty Malyshev), who also proposed the name that the church bears to this day – the Church of the Resurrection of Christ.

6. *Solovyev's attempt on the life of Alexander II in 1879.*

7. *The fatal explosion on 1 March 1881 that mortally wounded Alexander II.*

8. *The chapel near the Summer Garden, erected in memory of the salvation of the emperor on 4 April 1866 (later dismantled).*

9. *Konstantin Makovsky. Alexander II on his deathbed. 1881, Tretyakov Gallery, Moscow.*

10. *The consecration of the church. Procession around the Church of the Resurrection of Christ. South façade. 1907.*

11. *The consecration of the church. Procession around the Church of the Resurrection of Christ from the south side of the building. 1907.*

12. *Emperor Nicholas II greets the parade in honour of the consecration of the church. 1907.*

10

11

12

On 29 June 1883, the emperor accepted the basic proposals made by Parland and Father Ignatius, while requesting certain adjustments. The final version of the plans was approved on 1 May 1887. The ceremonial laying of the church's foundations took place on 6 October 1883. The excavations, construction and decoration of the church lasted a total of 24 years (1883–1907). The church was officially consecrated on 19 August 1907.

Alexander III was drawn to Parland and Father Ignatius' project by the fact that the architecture and ornamentation of the church involved certain techniques used in St Basil's Church in Moscow, which was considered a unique symbol of nationality in Russian art at the time. The Church on the Spilled Blood became the most striking example of the Neo-Russian style in architecture, which originated from the Orthodox traditions of church architecture. This style first emerged in Russia in the 1830s and reached its peak in the late 19th – early 20th century. Until recently, a negative opinion has been held of this interesting phenomenon in Russian architecture. It was largely disregarded because of negative criticism from art historians at the turn of the 20th century. Many buildings in the Neo-Russian style were ruthlessly destroyed, and the remainder, used for purposes other than those for which they were built and altered beyond recognition, quietly awaited their demise. It is all the more gratifying that these monuments are now unreservedly acknowledged by specialists who have now turned their attention to these buildings and rehabilitated them in the eyes of both society and the local authorities.

13. The Church of the Resurrection of Christ from Bank Bridge.

14

Thus, the Church on the Spilled Blood – one of Russia's most outstanding historic and artistic monuments – has regained its good name and former beauty.

When planning the Church of the Resurrection of Christ, the architects were faced with a difficult task: the spot on which the terrible deed had taken place was to be incorporated into the premises of the church. This explains its unusual

14. View of the north-west portico.

15. View of the south façade of the Church of the Resurrection of Christ from the Griboyedov (Catherine) Canal.

location on the very edge of the embankment. It is interesting to note that the usual technique of laying wooden foundations was rejected for the first time in favour of concrete foundations. The latter represented a technical innovation at the time and was the first construction experiment of its kind in Petersburg. Furthermore, in order to prevent the ground water and the waters from the nearby Catherine Canal from penetrating the building, the entire parameter of the church was sealed with a layer of clay.

Contemporaries viewed the Church of the Resurrection of Christ, reminiscent of the Moscow and Yarolsavl churches of the 16th and 17th centuries, as the embodiment of "national culture in all its historical uniqueness and significance". However, built with the aid of the latest advances in technology, the church was also rightly declared a "symbol of science": a progressive basic structure was effectively combined with archaic forms. Furthermore, not only the structure of the building, but its communications, heating and electrical systems too were created to the most modern standards.

The emergence of such a significant building in the historic centre of St Petersburg prompted the re-planning of its immediate environs. A paved square was laid around the church, a large part of which is surrounded by distinctive railings also designed by Parland. These are an interesting example of decorative metalwork in the Art Nouveau style. A wide bridge was raised across the canal and also constitutes a kind of continuation of the square.

16. Detail of the hipped roof of the south-west portico.

17. The Church of the Resurrection of Christ from Konyushenny Bridge.

The Church of the Resurrection of Christ has a single altar and three apses. The square body of the church is crowned with five cupolas: the central one sits atop a pointed roof and is surrounded by four onion-shaped domes. On the west side, a two-storey column-like bell tower adjoins the main body of the building. The church stands at a height of 81 metres and has a total area of 1,642.35 square metres. The Church on the Spilled Blood owes its architectural uniqueness and unusual structural design to the criteria that were laid down with regard to its creation. In order to erect the bell tower, which stands on the spot where the emperor was attacked, the body of the church was extended beyond the line of the embankment and thus juts into the canal. As a result, the building lacks symmetry and does not have the usual central entrance. Instead, it has two porches – one on either side of the bell tower – each with a sloping roof and a doorway leading into the church.

Its intricately decorated façades and stunning interior cause the church to resemble a rare and exotic flower blooming on the marshy lands of Petersburg. Artists, stonemasons, mosaicists, ceramists and enamellers were all involved in creating the monumental works that ornament the building.

The church is distinguished by its unusually refined décor. Most striking of all are the extravagant forms and bright colours of the distinctive cupolas, which, together with the spires of the Admiralty and the Peter and Paul Fortress and the golden dome of St Isaac's, are a dominant feature of the historic centre of Petersburg. It is the cupolas

18. Mosaic of "Christ in Glory" in the central arched gable of the south façade. Designed by Nikolai Koshelev.

18

19

20

21

that lend the face of the church the unique picturesque quality that makes it stand out amidst a panorama of buildings in the Classical style typical of the city.

The domes of the church are covered with gilded or enamelled sheets of brass. The decorative enamel covers an area of 1,000 square metres – an unprecedented phenomenon in the history of Russian architecture. The bell tower is also crowned with a gold cupola. The domes above the altar are covered with sheets of gilded brass, while the porches, cornices and pediments are decorated with zinc and brass.

The area around the base of the church is clad with grey Serdobol granite. The façade also boasts twenty slabs of dark red granite, bearing an account of the events that marked the reign of Alexander II. The walls are faced with red-brown Siegersdorf brick. Against this background, the ornamented casings, the arched gables decorated with mosaics, the ornamental bands, the inlays of glazed variegated brick, the colourful patterned tiles in the square cavities of the walls and the variegated tiles of the pointed roof and the roofs of the porches and apses seem all the more elegant. Particularly striking are the richly decorated arched gables of the north and south faces of the church. The red-brown of the masonry also enhances the harmonious combination of the carved marble columns, the colourful patterns of porcelain and ceramic bricks, and the mosaic illustrations in the tympanums.

The interior of the church is stunning for its profusion of Italian marble and rich assortment of Russian semiprecious stones as well as its textures and shades, not to mention a riot of mosaics, bronze and silver. The stone ornaments were created by master craftsmen from the Petersburg, Ekaterinburg and Kolyvan lapidary workshops.

The magnificent marble tiles on the floor of the church – the work of Italian masters – cover an area of 608 square metres. During the less fortunate years of the Church on the Spilled Blood's existence, this inlayed mosaic floor was almost completely destroyed, but it has since been restored to its former splendour. Before the revolution, it was protected by special carpets. Today, visitors to the church are only allowed to walk in designated areas.

19, 20. Mosaic of "Christ Giving the Blessing" in the central apse of the Church of the Resurrection of Christ. Designed by Alfred Parland.

21. Mosaic of "The Descent into Limbo" in the arched gable of the south porch of the south-west portico. Designed by Viktor Vasnetsov.

22. South-west portico.

Of particular artistic interest are the iconostasis, icon screens and canopy, executed in Italian marble, porphyry, rhodonite and jasper from the Ural and Altai Mountains. The iconostasis, which stands in front of the main altar and two smaller side altars, is decorated with Genoese marble and crowned with topaz crucifixes on gilded bronze mounts.

In the western part of the building, beneath the bell, a special canopy marks the spot of the tragedy. Here, seven steps below floor-level, one can see part of the street and railings of the former Catherine Canal – holy relics stained with blood from the time of the assassination. The canopy was created to designs by Parland and installed in July 1907. The images of the saints on the frieze were also based upon his sketches. The roof of the canopy consists of three rows of arched gables decorated with carvings and crowned with an eight-sided pyramid bearing a cross of 112 cut topazes. The vault of the canopy was inlayed with Bokhara azure, Siberian agate, jasper and topaz, cut in the form of stars.

However, it is the mosaics covering a vast area of the outer and inner walls (approximately 7,000 square metres in total) and executed with the utmost artistic and technical skill that make the church a monument of international significance. This unique collection of artworks, created by Russian and foreign firms, is unsurpassed elsewhere in Russia. The largest commission was received by the workshop of A. & V. Frolov, in which the majority of tessera works were executed. Talented Russian masters from the Mosaic Department of the Academy of Arts also played a part in bringing the various designs to fruition.

The decoration of the Church on the Spilled Blood was the first time in Russia that mosaics were used to such a large

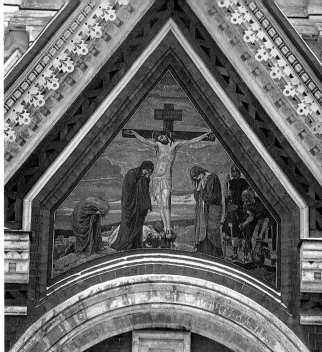

extent to ornament the outer walls of a church. The mosaics on the exterior cover a total area of over 400 square metres. Besides religious subjects, mosaic representations of the coats of arms of Russian towns and provinces cover three sides of the bell tower.

There is not a single painting inside the Church on the Spilled Blood: its walls are almost entirely covered with mosaics. When St Isaac's Cathedral was being decorated, it was decided to substitute paintings with mosaics because of the difficulty of creating an ideal climate inside the vast building.

23. Mosaic of "The Resurrection" in the central arched gable of the north façade. Designed by Mikhail Nesterov.

24. Mosaic of "The Saviour Borne by Angels in the Presence of the Virgin and St John" on the west façade. Designed by Mikhail Nesterov.

25. Mosaic of "The Bearing of the Cross" in the north arched gable of the north-west portico. Designed by Viktor Vasnetsov.

26. Mosaic of "The Crucifixion" in the west arched gable of the north-west portico. Designed by Viktor Vasnetsov.

27. Detail of the bell tower.

The builders of the Church on the Spilled Blood also chose to use this technique. The 308 mosaic illustrations inside the church, covering an area of 6,560 square metres, represent an enormous single item of artistic and cultural value. The panels created by the mosaicists from the Academy of Arts are distinguished by their technical excellence.

The designs for the mosaic decorations of the Church on the Spilled Blood were prepared by an entire group of artists, consisting of over 25 people. It was Parland's initial intention that all the mosaics in the church be created by one artist, namely Viktor Vasnetsov, who was already famed as an outstanding master of religious art. However, since Vasnetsov was working on other commissions at the time, he only produced sketches for two images now seen on the iconostasis – "The Saviour" and "The Mother of God and the Child" – and five mosaics on the outer walls: "The Bearing of the Cross", "The Crucifixion", "The Descent from the Cross"

28. Central nave.

*29. Mosaic of "Christ in Glory" in the main altar area.
Designed by Nikolai Kharlamov.*

30. Canopy.

and "The Descent into Limbo", which adorn the arched gables of the porches, and lastly "The Seraph".

Parland's second-choice artist after Vasnetsov was Andrei Ryabushkin. In his work, the latter was inspired by the traditions of Old Russian art. He designed 17 of the mosaics that decorate the inside of the church, including "The Healing of the Man with the Withered Hand", "Christ Heals a Boy with an Evil Spirit", "Christ Walking on the Waves" and "The Calling of the Apostle Matthew" on the north wall, "The Marriage at Cana" in the solea, "The Feeding of the Five Thousand" on the north vault, and others. He also produced sketches for seven of the mosaics that can be seen on the exterior of the church: "St Basil the Great", "St Vera", "St Igor", "St John the Baptist", "St Simon the Zealot", "Sts Boris and Gleb" and "Sts Mikhail of Chernigov and Fyodor the Boyar".

The highlight of the church's mosaic suite are the works of Nikolai Kharlamov. By that time, Kharlamov had earned just acclaim as a monumental artist who breathed new life into the canonical techniques of Byzantine art. He was entrusted with the task of designing subjects for the altar and the domes of the church. Kharlamov was responsible for 42 of the mosaics inside the church. The largest of these – "Christ the Pantocrator" on the roof of the central dome – is one of the artist's most famous works. Truly monumental, flat, devoid of excess colour and details, it is executed in the best traditions of Orthodox monumental art. The expressive, clearly defined visage of the Saviour exudes a powerful magnetism. The sublime spirituality and the extraordinary centripetal force

31. Mosaic of "The Eucharist" in the main altar area. Designed by Nikolai Kharlamov.

31

of the image make it the climax of the church's mosaic symphony. Yet another of Kharlamov's mosaics is to be found in the main altar area – "The Eucharist". This illustrates the liturgical subject of "The Last Supper", depicting the sacred nature of the rite of Communion (Eucharist), in contrast to the historical depictions that show the moment when Christ predicts His betrayal by Judas. In "The Eucharist" the Saviour offers the

32. Mosaic of "The Pantocrator" on the roof of the central dome. Designed by Nikolai Kharlamov.

33. Pillars under the dome as viewed from the canopy

holy bread to the disciples with His right hand ("Take, eat; this is my body"), while in His left hand he holds a cup of wine ("Take, drink; this is my blood of the covenant, which is poured out for many"). "John the Baptist" in the south-west dome, "The Mother of God" in the north-west dome and "Christ in Glory" in the altar are also the work of Kharlamov.

The outstanding Russian artist, Mikhail Nesterov, whose work is inextricably linked with the Russian Orthodox tradition, also designed a number of mosaics for the Church on the Spilled Blood. He made the preliminary preparations for the mosaic entitled "The Resurrection of Christ" in the

arched gable on the north façade of the church facing the Neva and for "The Saviour Borne by Angels in the Presence of the Virgin and St John" on the west façade above "The Crucifixion", executed according to designs by Parland. For the iconostasis, Nesterov designed the mosaics "The Ascension", "The Descent into Limbo", "The Holy Trinity", "Christ on the Road to Emmaus", the icon screens (commissioned by the Horse Guards Regiment) and the mosaics "St Alexander Nevsky" and "The Resurrection". The mosaic panels designed by Nesterov inside the church are distinguished by a particularly subtle combination of colours and shades.

34. Mosaic of "The Raising of the Son of the Widow of Nain" on the south-west pillar. Designed by Valerian Otmar.

35. Mosaic of "John the Baptist" on the vault of the south-west dome. Designed by Nikolai Kharlamov.

36. Mosaic of "The Sermon on the Mount" on the south vault. Designed by Vassily Belyaev.

35

36

Other famous Russian artists also involved in the mosaic ornamentation of the church included Belyaev, who designed the largest number of mosaics for the interior and exterior of the church (48 in total), Bodarevsky, Shakhovsky, and others.

The Church on the Spilled Blood, like the Church of Christ the Saviour in Moscow and St Isaac's Cathedral, was financed directly from the state coffers. Sermons were read daily, requiems

37. Mosaics of "The Angels Appearing to the Shepherds" and "The Nativity of Christ" on the south wall. Designed by I. Porfirov.

38. Mosaic of "The Entombment" on the west wall. Designed by Vassily Belyaev.

39. Mosaic of "The Blessing of the Children" on the solea. Designed by Vassily Belyaev.

37

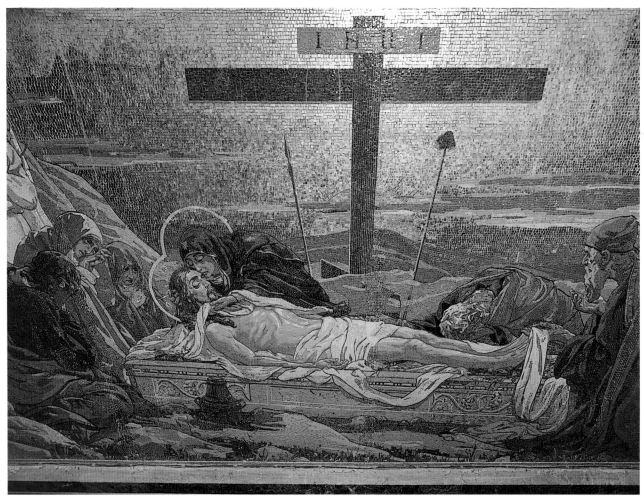

38

39

40

41

42

43

were performed and services were conducted in memory of Alexander II. Christenings, marriages and funerals, however, were not conducted, since this was not a parish church. A place

40. Mosaic of "St Alexander Nevsky" on the north icon screen. Designed by Mikhail Nesterov.

41. Mosaic of "The Angel Appearing to Joseph in a Dream" on the south wall. Designed by Valerian Otmar.

42. Mosaic of "The Saviour" on the central iconostasis. Designed by Viktor Vasnetsov.

43. Mosaic of "The Descent into Limbo" on the central iconostasis. Designed by Mikhail Nesterov.

44. Mosaic of "Mary Magdelene" on the north iconostasis. Designed by Nikolai Bodarevsky.

45. Mosaic of "Christ Driving the Money-changers from the Temple" on the solea. Designed by V. Pavlov.

44

45

near the west wall, in front of "The Resurrection", was set aside for the faithful, where church services were performed. After the revolution, the church was opened to all and services were held on a regular basis.

The Church on the Spilled Blood has always inspired a great deal of sentiment in St Petersburg. The atmosphere that surrounds the church by virtue of the reason for its existence and the beauty of its ornamentation has constantly drawn people to it from all over the country. On 30 October 1930, the authorities closed the church. It almost suffered the same fate as countless Orthodox churches throughout Russia, which were destroyed. For a number of years it was used as a warehouse like many other religious buildings in the city – the props from the Maly Theatre of Opera and Ballet were stored within its walls. Although the love of the faithful was unable to save the Church on the Spilled Blood from closure, the will of God preserved it from destruction during the siege, when a missile fell on the roof without exploding. The building was saved by the courage of a team of sappers who, under the direction of Viktor Demidov, risked their lives to defuse the missile in 1961. It is the skill and truly heroic efforts of the restorers, engineers and architects who worked on the renovation of the church that have made it possible for this unique work of art to bask once more in all its former glory, delighting viewers with its splendour. In 1970, a milestone in the history of the restoration of the church, the Church on the Spilled Blood became part of the State Museum "St Isaac's Cathedral". Complex technical works have been carried out to waterproof the building, repair the heating and ventilation systems and metallic structures, and to restore the monument's unique decorative fittings. Today, the restoration of the Church on the Spilled Blood is almost complete.

46. The Church of the Resurrection of Christ from the Mikhailovsky Garden.

47. The railings of the Mikhailovsky Garden around the Church of the Resurrection of Christ.

47

Mosaic of "The Crucifixion" on the west façade. Designed by Alfred Parland.

North façade of the Church of the Resurrection of Christ. —